KU-572-182

NATHAN W PYLE

STRANGE PLANET

WILDFIRE

FIRST PUBLISHED IN THE UNITED STATES IN 2019 BY
HARPERCOLLINS BOOKS.

FIRST PUBLISHED IN THE UK IN 2019 BY WILDFIRE,
AN IMPRINT OF THE HEADLINE PUBLISHING GROUP.

FIRST EDITION
DESIGNED BY NATHAN W. PYLE
ISBN 9781472269058

HEADLINE PUBLISHING GROUP, AN HACHETTE UK COMPANY,
CARMELITE HOUSE, 50 VICTORIA EMBANKMENT, LONDON, EC4Y0DZ
WWW.HEADLINE.CO.UK
WWW.HACHETTE.CO.UK

TO TAYLOR:

YOU REMOVE THE AIR
FROM MY LUNGS

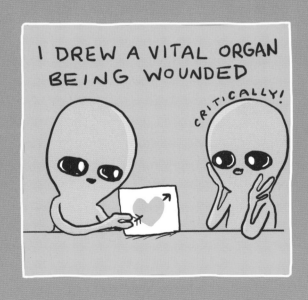

IMAGINE PLEASANT NONSENSE

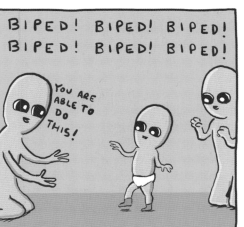

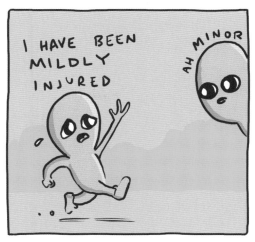

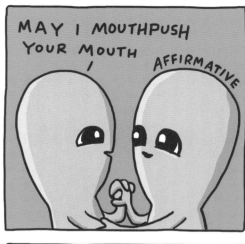

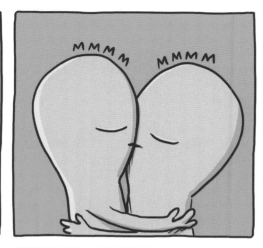

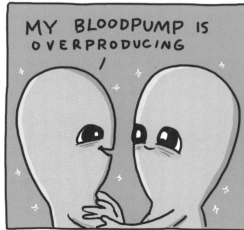

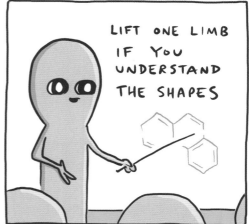

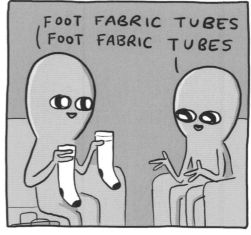

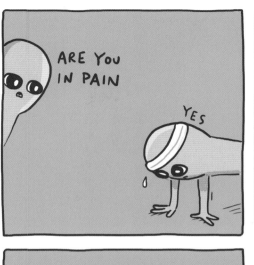

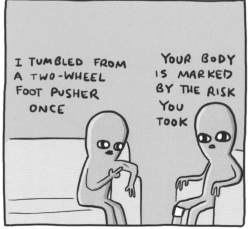

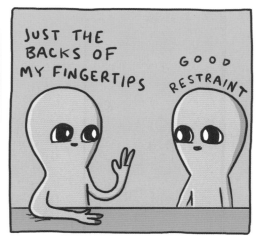

TOMORROW WE AWAKE PRE-STAR FOR STRENUOUS ACTIONS

A REGRETTABLE AGREEMENT

BUT THIS MACHINE'S GENTLE TONES WILL ALERT US TO RISE

A SOOTHING MELODY

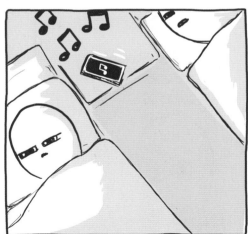

I WISH TO HARM THE MELODY MACHINE

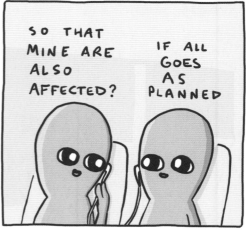

IDENTIFY YOURSELF! I AM HOLDING RECREATIONAL EQUIPMENT!

I AM GOING TO HAPHAZARDLY SWING THIS OBJECT

SHALL I ACCOMPANY

YOU ARE SAFER HERE GIVEN WHAT I JUST SAID

OK I PREFER THIS PLAN

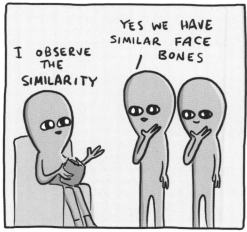

THE CREATURE HAS VISITED SEVERAL TIMES

I PROPOSE WE PROMOTE IT TO PERMANENT STATUS IN OUR HOME

WE SHOULD CAREFULLY CONSIDER THIS SINCE WE JUST MET THIS CREATURE

TRUE - WE OUGHT TO ASK THE CREATURE WHAT IT WANTS

THE CREATURE WANTS TO BE OUR BEST FRIEND

WE WILL PLAN OUR SCHEDULE AROUND THIS CREATURE

ADULTHOOD

DIFFICULT DAY YET I MAINTAIN COMPOSURE

HA THIS SMALL SETBACK AMUSES ME

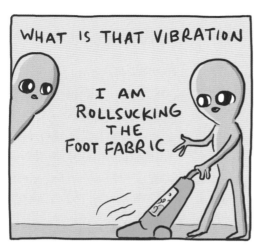

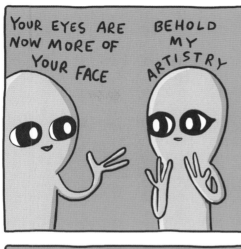

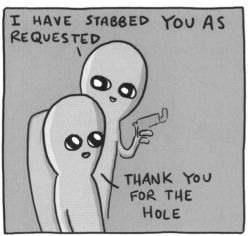

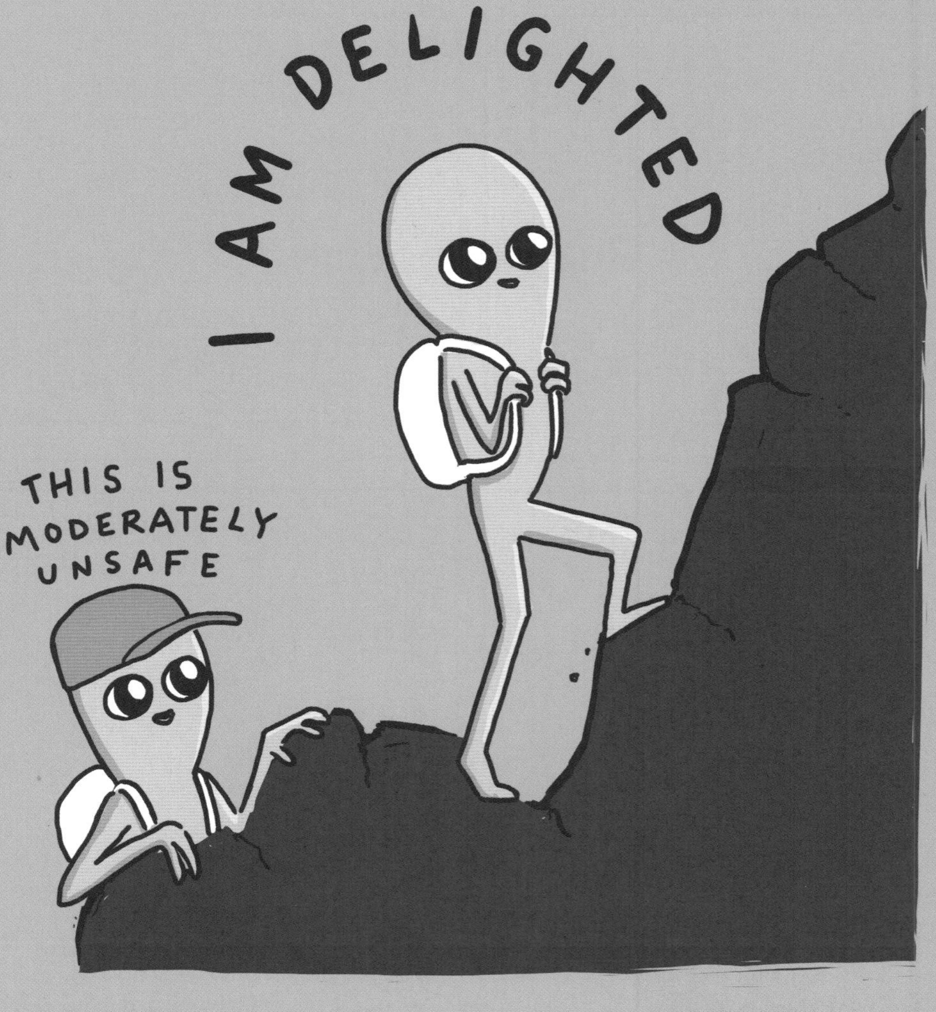
I AM DELIGHTED
THIS IS MODERATELY UNSAFE

THE GROUP OF ORB CATCHERS THAT REPRESENT OUR REGION DID NOT CATCH THE ORB TONIGHT

THIS WAS DISAPPOINTING BUT WE ARE GRATEFUL FOR THEIR EFFORT

AND THOUSANDS OF BEINGS STILL WORE SUPPORTIVE HATS AS THEY WENT HOME SAD

THANK YOU - THAT IS NICE TO HEAR ABOUT THE HATS

ORBS

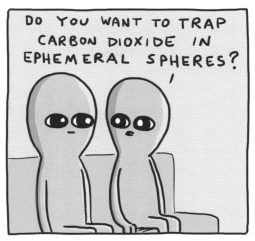

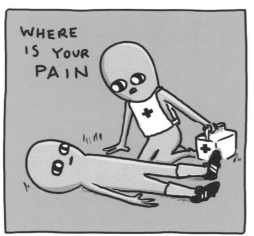

COMMONLY OBSERVED OBJECTS

PERSONAL STAR DIMMERS

SERIOUSNESS CLOTH

ORB CATCHER HAT

FOOT RAMPS

FOOT FABRIC TUBES

STAND-UP RINSE OFF

MOUTH STONE BRUSH

MOUTH STONE GOO

LEAF SMELL

FORCE STRING

COMMONLY OBSERVED OBJECTS

HYDRATION
CYLINDER

EXCESS
FUNGUS
SLICES

VAST
DOUGH
CIRCLE

LEAFBUCKET

HOT LEAF
LIQUID

TWICE HEATBLASTED
DOUGHSLICE

SWEET DISKS

CRISS CROSS
FLOP DISK

JITTER
LIQUID

PLANT LIQUID
PARTIALLY DIGESTED
BY INSECTS
AND THEN STOLEN